SPORNO!

SPORNO!
WHEN SPORT GETS A BIT DIRTY

JOSH BURT

SIMON &
SCHUSTER

London · New York · Sydney · Toronto · New Delhi

A CBS COMPANY

First published in Great Britain by Simon & Schuster UK Ltd, 2013
A CBS Company

3 5 7 9 10 8 6 4 2

Simon & Schuster UK Ltd
1st Floor
222 Gray's Inn Road
London WC1X 8HB

www.simonandschuster.co.uk

Simon & Schuster Australia,
Sydney

Simon & Schuster India,
New Delhi

Photographs © Getty Images

A CIP catalogue record for this book is
available from the British Library

ISBN 978-1-47112-906-3
Ebook ISBN 978-1-47112-907-0

Designed by Jacqui Caulton

Printed and bound in Italy by
L.E.G.O. S.p.A. Vicenza

Introduction

Back at the very dawn of time, early man had basically two things on his mind: hurtling around vast landscapes with a club chasing things, and tenderly performing various instinctive and sensual sex acts on his lover. Or, to modernise these activities and put them in layman's terms: sport and porn. They were the only two primal pleasures that came completely naturally, and could be carried out despite early man's inability to communicate beyond the word 'ug' and his absolutely tiny caveman mind.

Evolution has been kind to that guy. Nowadays, where once there were uncomfortable animal skins, now he can nip to Marks & Spencer where he'll find wonderful outfits in their 'leopard-print clothes' aisle; where once he'd have been required to slaughter a wild animal for his dinner, now supermarkets do all that for him. I'm not entirely sure where I'm going with this, except to say that while the world has turned zillions of times and the landscape has changed in every which way, those two constants remain: man's lust for sport, and his lust for sex.

Of course, there is no concrete statistical evidence to back this up, and I'm not a doctor, but I'd suspect that exactly the same concoction of hormones and chemicals that rush around your body when you're kicking a ball about are probably the same heady cocktail present when you're banging that special someone on the bathroom floor. That's just a hunch. Marinate on that.

Anyway, all of this leads very seamlessly to *Sporno!* – that small world that exists right in the middle of the Venn diagram that finds sport and porn overlapping. You could miss these moments in the blink of an eye. But thankfully these days, with thousands of cameras trained on every sportsperson at every sporting event, the previously overlooked relationship between sport and porn has finally been realised in book form.

Delve in, peruse, study. Here you'll find photographs of athletes being tender with one another, angry exchanges seemingly spilling over into emotional make-up sex, those stolen moments when a man or woman finds themselves alone in the middle of a football pitch with an erection (or a woman's version of an erection) and no place to go. You'll find positions you didn't even know existed until now.

Enjoy what lies ahead. There really are some magnificent pictures waiting for you, and in the words of the great philosopher Socrates: it's Sporno, ladies and gentlemen!

SPORNO!

Behind the Striker

The world's second greatest player, Cristiano Ronaldo, is impressive both on and off the pitch. This is him training for his off-the-pitch lifestyle.

Back Pass

You'd need the world's biggest magnifying glass to pick up all the off-the-ball incidents in a typical game of football – nudges here, insults there, a couple of players having a quick bum behind the ref's back. Observe: Exhibit A.

Backline Spritz

Rugby is a brutal sport that dates back to absolutely ages ago
– possibly the Iron Age, definitely Roman times, which is why
you'll occasionally see moves clearly more suited to one of
Emperor Caligula's weeknight sex orgies.

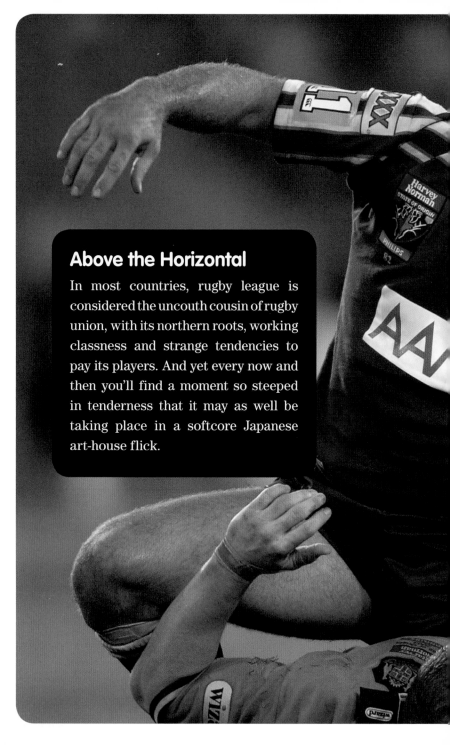

Above the Horizontal

In most countries, rugby league is considered the uncouth cousin of rugby union, with its northern roots, working classness and strange tendencies to pay its players. And yet every now and then you'll find a moment so steeped in tenderness that it may as well be taking place in a softcore Japanese art-house flick.

Two Guys One Bike

Look at the French cyclists Jimmy Casper and Arnaud Coyot dicking around at the Tour de France. Go on, look at them. Just look at them. Keep looking. Keep looking. Now look away. And now look again.

What the Shaq!

In a frankly upsetting display of weird sportsmanship, this photo finds the legendary baller Shaquille O'Neal smearing a dirty great big smudge on his good reputation by 'mounting' the opposition.

Anaconda Choke

Clamber into that UFC ring, and you'll see thumping, spanking, gouging, stroking, kissing, kicking, cupping, licking and in the case of this haunting image, you'll see two men caught up in the most primal moment of all time.

Slam Dunk

Kobe Bryant is adored, revered and held in the kind of esteem normally reserved for presidents of the United States, kings of Nova Scotia, or messiahs sent from heaven. In some cases, you could say he's a little bit too adored by the opposition, if you catch my drift.

Stud's Up

Back in the olden days when David Beckham played in sunny Spain and Owen Hargreaves was just your typical curly-haired German lad with a soft Canadian accent, this happened. This was the moment when women all over the world suddenly wanted to be Owen Hargreaves.

Making the Tackle

This move dates back to before evolution even really began, and it features in every single sport known to man. It's a simple logic: if they're getting away, grab their dick. It's known in the trade as 'making the tackle'.

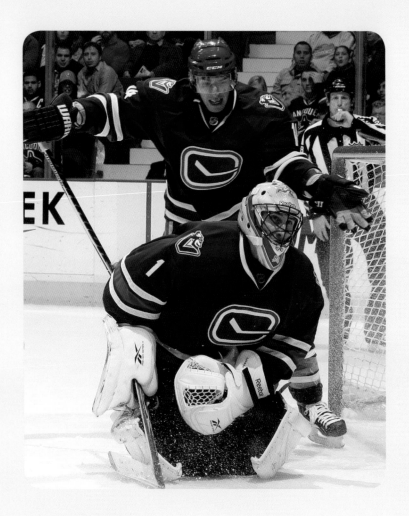

The Other Puck

Ice hockey is brutal, fast, sensual, erotic and sexy. This picture finds Roberto Luongo and Alex Burrows practising something which is often found depicted in magazines that you might find in a hedge or underneath your granddad's bed.

Huggo Bonito

You'll remember Roberto Carlos as the cheeky left back who once scored a preposterous goal that started four and a half miles wide of the bottom right-hand corner and ended up turning back on itself in mid air and scorching into the top left. It was a fluke he then attempted to repeat at least twenty times a game for the rest of his career. In the above picture he's not doing that for once. Instead, he's massaging his friend Ronaldo's lovely bum using his groin.

The Shag

When it kicks off in the ring, you'd better shield the kids' eyes because it kicks off big time. Men, leotards, baby oil making their muscles shine – there's only one way this is heading.

Froggy Style

A moving moment from the London Olympics, as two wrestlers become one. If you were to add a nice Righteous Brothers track and some mood lighting, this could easily be a love scene from *Ghost*.

Splash and Grab

There's a saying in life: what happens in Vegas stays in Vegas. That could equally apply to what happens underwater, because here it's very obvious indeed what's going on and should never be spoken about. Not ever.

The Grateful Lady

Back near the beginning of this millennium, the gorgeous Spanish defender Sergio Ramos plucked a goal celebration from the anals, sorry, from the annals of time that hadn't been seen for quite a while. It's known only as 'the grateful lady'.

The Indiscreet Waz

Wayne Rooney is practically royalty in the UK, so screw you, he can do what the hell he likes – even if that means dropping to the ground for bit of solo fun on the training pitch, while wearing a garish cycling proficiency top.

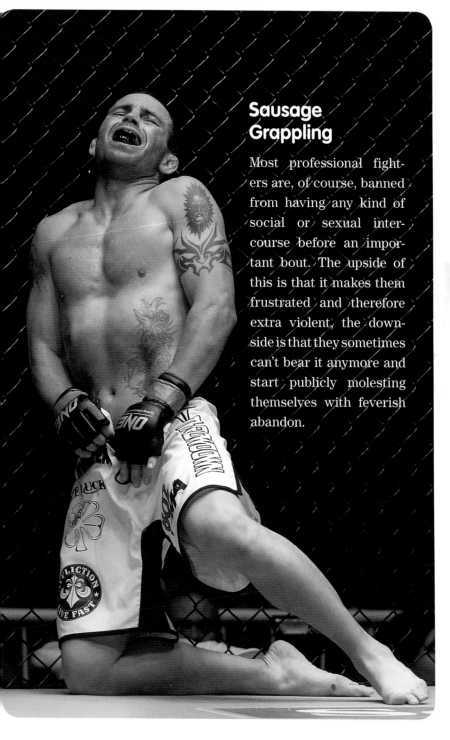

Sausage Grappling

Most professional fighters are, of course, banned from having any kind of social or sexual intercourse before an important bout. The upside of this is that it makes them frustrated and therefore extra violent, the downside is that they sometimes can't bear it anymore and start publicly molesting themselves with feverish abandon.

Solo Effort

Ask your grandfather and he'll tell you all about the early 1960s – it wasn't all free love and dope smoking just yet, he'd tell you, sometimes mid-match orgasms were still strictly to be enjoyed alone. Yeah, okay, Granddad.

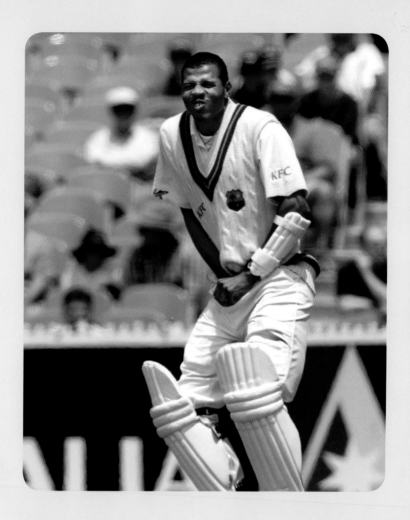

The Flipper

Cricket is a game so slow, so tense and so boring that sometimes you just need to thrust your hand down into your whites and unwind the organic way. Like Mervyn Dillon from a place called Mission Village is doing here – what would the clergy have to say about this?

Vulving

Professional pole-vaulters are perpetually reinventing techniques, so where they used to just use the spring from their heels and the strength in their arms, now they might use their amazing washboard stomachs or their outlandishly strong vaginas.

Stroke Two

In baseball you'll find players combining numerous behavioural rituals like they've got OCD. They'll chew, spit, punch their gloves, rub their genitals, chew, spit, touch their genitals again, keep touching their genitals, wink an eye, back to genitals, stay on the genitals, keep rubbing the genitals and on and on.

Hurdler's Cock

The problem with those high hurdles is that every time you jump over one you smash a bit of your privates right into the middle of it. It smarts like mad. Here's LaShawn Merritt basically saying sorry to his dick.

Courtside Relief

In the olden days before film cameras were erected in sports arenas to stop anyone from nicking the gaffer's wallet, it was easy to conceal a private moment of tension relief during a basketball match. Those days are long gone, but someone obviously didn't get the memo.

CollingWOOD

Sportsmen don't just love what they do, they adore it with the kind of passion most of us save for things like missionary intercourse or doggy-style intercourse. For the flame-haired former England run machine Paul Collingwood, even just practising cricket is a massive turn-on.

Self Maul-estation

The giant Frenchman Sebastian Chabal didn't dance to the same beat as everyone else, hence the long womanly hair

and the big bushy fisherman's beard. Not to mention the numerous times he'd plonk himself down mid-match and start having a wank.

Sticky Wicket

The England and Warwickshire batsman Jonathan Trott is one of cricket's most straight-faced and thorough players, and this picture demonstrates exactly how he likes to deal with a 'sticky wicket' during the middle of an innings. It's quite shocking, actually.

Hodd's Bod (or Hoddle's Boddle)

As if he didn't have enough going for him with his salon standard hairstyles, his natural touch and his divine footballing ability, it turns out that Glenn Hoddle also had an Adonis body. No wonder jealous England managers absolutely hated him.

The Sexy Ronald

Ronnie O'Sullivan is snooker's most naturally gifted player blah blah blah, he can play with his left hand yada yada yada. He's also really sexy when he sticks his tongue out and licks his lips.

Peek-a-Boo

One legendary tactic among heavyweight boxers is to trick your opponent into doubting your toughness by sending them love poems and pictures of you with cute animals, like rabbits or donkeys. World champion Lennox Lewis was notoriously good at this in his day.

Ice Packing

Hey Arsenal fans, look at this beautiful picture of Alan Smith moistening his inner thighs just for you (but mainly himself).

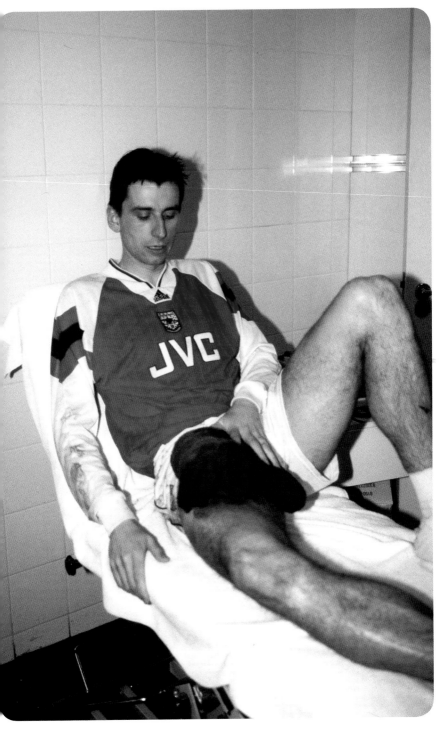

Advantage Williams

In tennis, you sometimes need to try anything to get the crowd on your side. Andre Agassi used to slowly shave his chest to

make chicks fancy him. In Paris, Venus Williams thought the best way to go about it was to look as though she was not wearing any knickers.

Blind Man's Chuff

When he's not hurtling towards swimming pools from great heights, Tom Daley likes to relax by popping on a blindfold and seeing how the evening pans out from there.

Snatch Point

There are strict dress codes at Wimbledon which allow a gentlewoman only to flash the small piece of flesh above her elbow or a little bit of her ankle, so when it comes to the rest of the tour the ladies like to go absolutely wild. Remember 2002? The year Serena Williams wore bondage gear at a tournament? Course you do.

The Wet Look

While a walking race sounds like an oxymoron, don't be fooled: these chicks work up one hell of a sweat when they get going. Look at the fast walker Maria Czakova, she's literally wet T-shirting herself, the minx.

A Ladylike Gift

These days, footballers have no idea how to woo one another before the big game: no foreplay, no lapdancing, no sweet vocal runs from Frank Lampard or Cristiano Ronaldo, despite

both of them having voices like angels. It's not like the old days when Russian guys would turn up at a Chelsea match with a nice bunch of flowers for their hosts. Now they just buy the club instead.

Banter

Those summer Olympics: Emeli Sandé, Usain Bolt – and the British heptathlete girls hiding behind a Union flag and whipping their tops off for the barking paparazzi. Great times.

Large Cox

The thrill of picking up a bronze medal affects people in different ways. Some are moved to tears, some can't stop smiling, some get enormous hard-ons.

The Full Monty

The Haka is now considered to be the throwing down of a gauntlet, a violent, unruly ode to competitiveness. But did you know that about a hundred years ago it was far more pelvic and suggestive and was performed to stripping music? Well now you do.

One In, One Out

This is gradually becoming commonplace after a long cycling race, and basically involves one guy getting attended to while the other one handles any probing questions about what kind of helmets are best or how to fix a puncture.

Victorious Sand Hugging

With victory comes a hormonal surge that can blow a woman's mind, so when Misty May-Treanor and Kerri Walsh Jennings won the gold at the recent Olympics it took a cameraman roughly 0.8 nanoseconds before his lens was navigating their bodies like they were something you'd mention in a smutty metaphor about navigation.

Picture This

Basketball is very stop-starty, so there's a real emphasis on keeping the crowd constantly entertained, be it with a dancing mascot, some cheerleaders with great bums that fans can stare longingly at, a get-it-in-the-basket competition, or just a nice sexual showcase from one of the players for the many photographers lining the court.

A Phwoar Pointer

As with all sport, sometimes it's what you do when you're not in possession of the ball that can win or lose a match. Here Kwame Brown is engaging in the renowned art of 'distraction' by brazenly urging the opposition to have a look at his junk.

The Missionary Position

It's important to limber up when you're an athlete. Stretch your arms, stretch your legs, pop yourself down on the track and spread-eagle your wondrous thighs as you might just before going at it hammer and tongs with a lover.

Team Meating

If an ice hockey team is in disarray, it's the moment to call time-out so you can huddle together and replenish your team spirit with a quick game of Cock or Ball.

Grabbing Johnson

When the US 4x400 side trounced the world record in
the late 1990s, two men met groin-on in wild celebration.
One was Michael Johnson. The other was not.

Patting

Here the Crystal Palace goalie Paul Barron is making his colleague feel special by rubbing his lovely bottom and whispering some kind words directly into his right ear. That's great keeping and even better team bonding.

Affectionate Holding

Shoulder pads, tight-fitting uniforms outlining every curve, bulge, or layer of warm cellulite spread across the back of your thighs. Yes sir, American football couldn't be more manly if it grew a beard and started shouting 'Charge!'

Congratulatory Hand Shake

Back in the 1960s – when free love was rife and everyone would just kill time by shagging each other – it was common courtesy to mutually loosen your competitor's valve after a big race. In a manner of speaking, in that valve means penis and loosen means touch.

Holding One Another

Like every workout needs a cooling-off period, so water polo players need to untangle their muscular knots after a big game by rubbing one another's backs, kissing their eyelids, generally 'holding one another'.

Beach Bundle

More commonly located in honeymoon suites or in the back of caravans up by the Point, the traditional one-on-one 'beach

bundle' always starts off innocently enough, but then pretty soon you'll be doing it on rocks or in caves. Or on car bonnets in front of other people. For money.

A Moment in Time

There is no name for this kind of thing. No rhyme, nor reason. It just is.

Spine Tingler

Wrestling is a complex sport that can take you down numerous different alleyways, depending on your opponent's strengths and weaknesses. In this case, the guy in blue is using an ancient seduction technique to startle his rival. It seems to be working.

The Horizontal Spike

In any team sport from time to time a whisper of congratulations and a pat on what the Brits would call 'the dick' will be required to gee up your teammate. Or you could just lie down legs akimbo and go at it for a bit. Note how the cameraman doesn't get in quite as close as he does for the women's beach volleyball. Funny, that.

One in the Hole

Golf at its best combines both mental and physical skills. Mental skills to keep you awake, physical skills to stop your hands from trembling uncontrollably. One way to beat the shakes is with a quick shag next to some long grass.

Short Disposal

Sometimes the wafer-thin line between sport and foreplay blurs on the field of play, like in this picture which finds Aussie Rules man Nick Dal Santo unsure of whether to kick for points or sod that and just go straight to third base.

A Clean Finish

Once you've pulled on your latex swimsuit, oiled up your boobs a treat and crawled into the wrestling ring for a massive

fight with another woman, pretty much anything goes. In this picture one lady is marking her arrival by using a move called a 'clean finish'.

A Fancy Man's Banquet

Sometimes common courtesy flies out of the window when you're in pursuit of a gold medal and all that's left are random karate chops and groin work. But that's Greco-Roman wrestling for you.

Semi-Bookended

Thanks to some much-needed changes to the law, you won't see anyone fully bookended these days, but this picture finds one half of the process being executed with textbook skill by the handsome Argentine striker Carlos Tevez. See how Rio Ferdinand squirms with humiliation? That's gotta smart!

Saliva Swapping

Where once it was traditional to end a football match by seductively removing your shirt and passing it to the opposition player you most fancy, nowadays some players raise a finger to foreplay and go straight for the snog.

Two Love

Once a hard-fought match is done, thank your opponent however you like: shake their hand, do a high five, bump fists, show one another your balls. If you're a couple of hot chicks, by all means start making out.

Tongue Slalom

Like with Stockholm Syndrome, professional athletes can fall in love inappropriately. Only, instead of bearded men holding flick knives and machine guns, these guys get a thing for their equipment. Look at skier Tina Maze smooching her ski like it's a person. She's obviously gone completely insane.

Gary's Kiss

How do you celebrate a goal? By sliding on your knees? Do you do a little Salsa with the corner flag? Manchester United right-back Gary Neville used to search out Paul Scholes for a nice kiss on the mouth.

A Cheeky Kiss

Basketball is bloody intense, man. You've got to bounce the ball, you've got to throw it at the hoop, you've got to deal with some pretty unruly language. Not to mention the massive Chinese guys hitting on you 24/7.

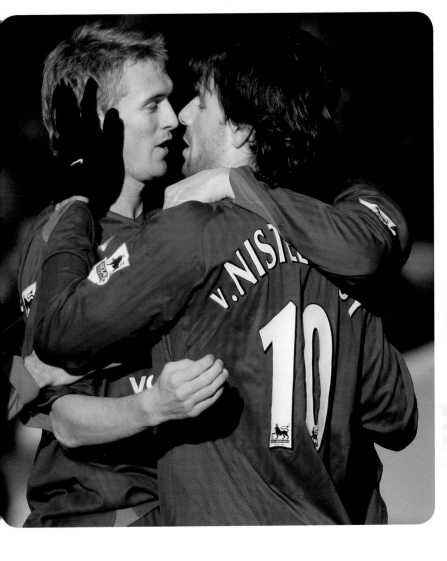

Ruud Awakening

Like Gary Neville and Paul Scholes, Ruud van Nistelrooy and Darren Fletcher have been spotted closing their eyes for a tender moment after a goal, only Ruud likes to incorporate some extra face-stroking into proceedings.

Slaven's Reward

To be a good football manager you need to get the fans on your side either by inspiring your team to some decent results, or else by greeting them when they invade the pitch with a gentle kiss on the mouth, which could even go full French depending on the mood.

The Big Decision

Two men, one moment: do they follow their hearts? Their groins? Or do they get up and start shouting random swearwords at the ref? The Earth briefly stopped spinning on its axis that day.

The Nude Intruder

The 2002 Tri Nations encounter between Australia and New Zealand will be remembered mainly as the match where some naked dude ran onto the pitch and everything got a bit steamy. The usual hymn singing was momentarily replaced by wah wah guitars and moaning sounds.

Heavy Petting

Even during the heat and intensity of the 1970 FA Cup final replay, Chelsea legend Peter 'The Cat' Bonetti wasn't averse to getting his fur tickled.

Chelsea Style

When it comes to the relationship between Lamps and JT, there are no boundaries, they're literally in each other's DNA, whatever that means. The above picture finds them toasting another great success in their usual fashion.

Man Down

One popular celebration over in Italy is for a Frenchman to fall
to his knees in subservience to his captain – most frequently
the popular AC Milan defender Alessandro Costacurta. This
dates back to 1423 when something happened to make this
a tradition.

The Gaffer's Want

In the wild, primates can be observed perpetually hammering home their dominance by beating each other up, or demanding sexual gratification as a show of respect. Of course, by 'in the wild' we obviously mean 'at football clubs' and by 'primates' we probably mean 'people'. And by 'people' we mean 'Jose Mourinho' and by 'primates' we also mean 'Frank Lampard'. This is all getting very confusing.

Sliding Tackle

Definitely one of the most handsome human beings of all time, when he's not standing naked in front of full-length mirrors or imagining who'd win a hotness competition between him and George Clooney, Paolo Maldini allows people to rub his legs. Trained people. With certificates.

Banana Man

When he's not doing lovely chips onto the green or smashing one hell of a wallop onto the fairway, Ian Poulter likes to slowly seduce the crowd by working a banana with his mouth.

Number 6.9

Figure skating is peppered with difficult moves, few more so than 'number 6.9', which involves each partner peering awkwardly at one another's willies and vaginas while still gliding round and round in a perfect circle. Tends to score highly.

Cherry-pop

To stand out as a figure skater these days, you have to pull something recognisable but unconventional out of the bag. Like this, which Margarita Drobiazko and Povilas Vanagas saw being done in a cage at Manumission and decided to turn into an ice-skating move.

The Happy Swans

This sassy US pairing certainly know their way around a difficult figure-skating move, and they don't come much trickier than this one, which can simultaneously draw gasps from the audience and a round of applause from people who are generally excellent in bed.

X-rated Challenge

Classic poolside horseplay from Brazil's luxury player Robinho here. He's being all like 'you can't get with this', while his international teammate Elano is like: 'Screw you, man. I could TOTALLY get with that.'

Team Formation

Team bonding here as the German midfielder Michael Ballack is explaining the events of a quiet night in to his colleague Per Mertesacker. By the looks of things, he had sex using his massive penis.

Caretaker Manager

Compared to Arsène Wenger's whispered instructions containing zero eye contact and his soft, congratulatory handshakes if you scored a goal, Spain would have been an incredible culture shock for Thierry Henry. This depicts one of the few Barcelona training sessions where you get to wear clothes.

Standing Spoon

At the 1998 World Cup, tensions were running high in the Italian camp, so Christian Vieri and his training pal Moreno Torricelli often found their happy place the good old-fashioned way.

Ball-up

With so much riding on their careers, sportsmen will stretch the boundaries of human decency to guarantee a spot on the team. In this picture the Aussie Rules player Fraser Gehrig is quite clearly showing his goods to his coach for some daft reason.

Caught Behind

To be a professional quick bowler, you need to understand the contours of the human body so you can premeditate movement. Here the Australian quickie Peter Siddle gets to grips with the protruding 'arse' area of a batsman.

Getting Treatment

After regularly firing down 100mph deliveries, fate decrees that sometimes it should be Shoaib Akhtar's turn to feel the full force of a gentleman's hand. Here he's definitely feeling the full force of a gentleman's something.

Caddyshag

There's an age-old saying about how golf can ruin a lovely romantic walk, but that's bullshit, man. Look around you – you've got bunkers to lie down in, trees to hide behind. Tell you what, you could cuddle a guy behind some of those trees.

A Back Barn Burner

Calming down a boxer after a big fight can be a gruelling, lengthy and quite boring process, so in this case super lightweight fighter Randall Bailey's warm-down is being hurried along using a technique more commonly associated with vets.

Getting Treatment

Modern tennis – you've got the crowd on your back, your coach eye-scolding you whenever you make a mistake, sometimes you just need a brisk hand job in between points. Right, guys?

Trackside Relief

Back at the last London Olympics before the ones in 2012 it was the sight of a Swedish 800m athlete having all manner of a great time trackside that caused a sharp intake of breath. Not Danny Boyle's amazing opening ceremony.

Body Checking

'Body Checking' is commonplace in ice hockey. It either means another player just slammed you into a board, or that some member of the public arrived from nowhere to rifle around your underpants for a laugh. This picture shows Option 2.

Touch Rugby

Sweet fancy Moses! Is that guy milking Bill Young like a cow? Oh no, don't worry, apparently he's just monkeying around with his naughty bits. Sorry Bill!

Middle Stump

Professional cricketers like to use all kinds of protective apparatus to maintain the wellbeing of their private parts, with the possible exception of the Australia skipper Michael Clarke, here boasting about going commando.

Rugby Tackle

In rugby league there are no rules. Okay, there are lots of rules, but there isn't one that says you can't remove an opponent's

shorts for a quick look at what he might be packing. Or there might be. No one knows.

Rucking With Your Shorts Off

The origin of this ritual is lost in the mists of time; we are unsure whether it stems from the Northern Hemisphere, the Southern Hemisphere or from one of the many other hemispheres that people are always going on about. But the trick is to throw your opponents by arriving at a ruck with your arse out for some reason.

More Rucking With Your Shorts Off

Here's another example of a man arriving at a ruck situation with his shorts practically around his ankles. The results are twofold: either the opposition becomes 'uncomfortable', or they get 'horny'. Some are known to get both.

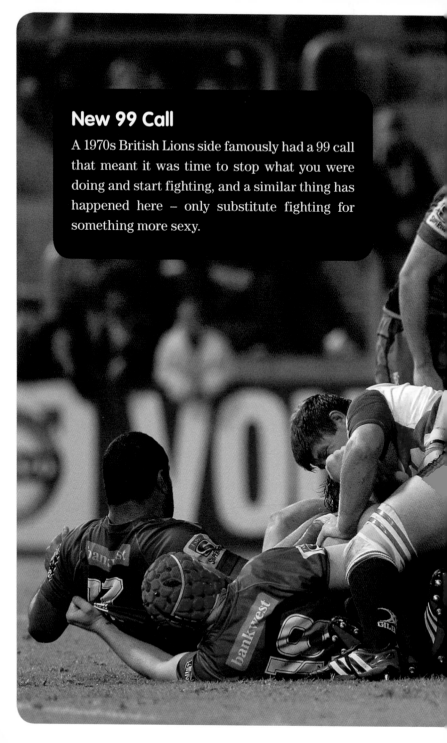

New 99 Call

A 1970s British Lions side famously had a 99 call that meant it was time to stop what you were doing and start fighting, and a similar thing has happened here – only substitute fighting for something more sexy.

Rafa's Break

At the end of a tough match, sometimes you just have to bite down on the first thing you can get your hands on.

The Missionary Position

No one truly knows how to react to Super Bowl victory until it happens. Some might feel empty inside, some might be inspired to dance, Ryan Clark of the Pittsburgh Steelers likes to assume the missionary position.

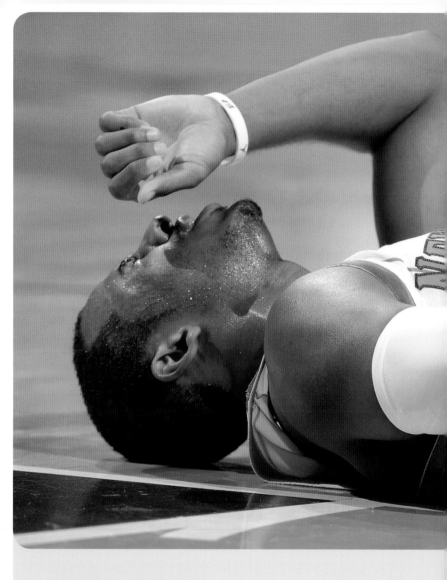

Injuring your Groin

As everyone knows, there's a difference between injuring your groin and 'injuring your groin'. This picture finds basketball's Chris Paul definitely injuring his groin.

Putting on a Show(er)

All swimming baths give you the choice – lather up publicly in front of onlookers, or exercise discretion and hunt down a cubicle. The diver Tom Daley regularly goes public because he's uber-confident about his bikini line.

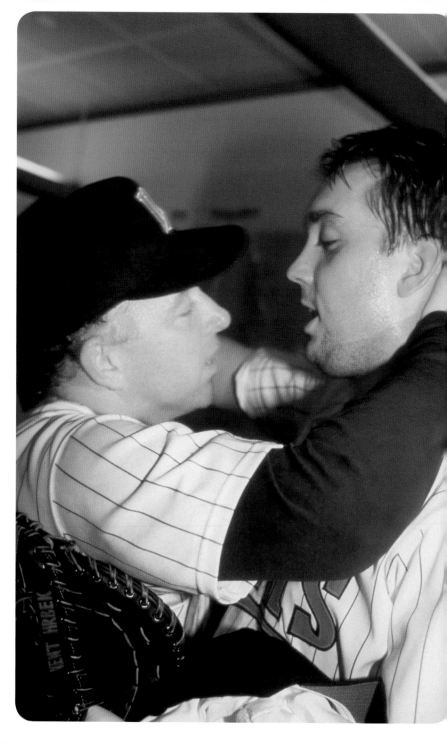

The Textbook Lunge

Because the head rush from winning a trophy is probably identical to the feeling you get when you're about to enjoy foreplay with a stripper, it's easy to get confused and attempt to passionately kiss your colleagues.

First Base

Sometimes the air is so thick with anxiety, there's only one thing to do – just get the guy on the loud speaker to tell the crowd to look away first.

Copping a Feel

Dating back to the 1950s, when guys in leather jackets would pat girls' bums for sport, this move literally never fails. Okay, that's a lie; it frequently fails. The point is this... nope, there is no point. It's just a guy feeling another guy's bottom.

Face Mounting

The fighting community is extremely close knit, so every once in a while the act of passionately punching someone repeatedly in the face can morph into something a little bit steamier.

Standing Spoons

Look at these strong immovable basketball stars stealing a moment of tenderness during a game. Anyone not currently in floods of tears needs to see a doctor about not having a heart.

The Careless Whisper

The list of methods used to stop your opponent is long and quite boring, but about midway down you'll find the subsection about 'distraction' and in that there are a few words about caressing his or her buttocks as they run away from you.

Splash and Dash

Motor racing is seriously intense, with all the shouting from the stands and the hot girls in tiny little outfits, so once on the podium drivers like to let of steam the old-fashioned way. Rather than outlaw this behaviour, the powers-that-be just turn a blind eye and discuss the weather for a bit.

Game, Set, got a Match?

After any exercise marathon, there's only one thing for it –
crack out the cigs. Go on, you deserve it.